Celebrated Virtuosic Solos

Nine Exciting Solos for Early Intermediate/Intermediate Pianists

Robert D. Vandall

Everyone who plays the piano wants to play a piece that is impressive to an audience. Pianists are drawn to those pieces that challenge them to quickly move their fingers, hands and arms, creating sounds that move the audience to respond with wild applause and shouts of "Bravo!"

The pieces in the *Celebrated Virtuosic Solos* are meant to show off the athleticism, as well as the musicality, of the performer. My hope is that these pieces will excite students, teachers and audiences alike.

Enjoy!

Robert D. Vandall

Contents

Allegretto Scherzando 16

Allegro in A Minor 19

Billowing Breakers 6

Handbell Joy 12

Mystical Tarantella 22

Perpetual Motion III 9

Scale Train 4

Summer Toccatina 2

Triad Toccatina 14

Copyright © MMVII by Alfred Publishing Co., Inc.
All rights reserved.   Printed in USA.
ISBN-10: 0-7390-4666-7
ISBN-13: 978-0-7390-4666-1

Summer Toccatina

Robert D. Vandall

Scale Train

Robert D. Vandall

Billowing Breakers

Robert D. Vandall

Perpetual Motion III

Robert D. Vandall

10

Handbell Joy

Robert D. Vandall

Triad Toccatina

Robert D. Vandall

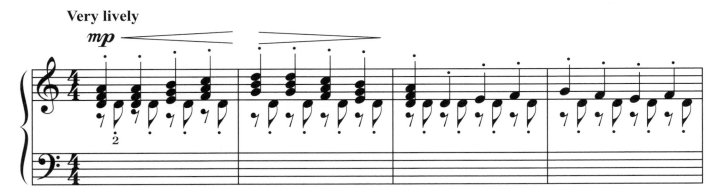

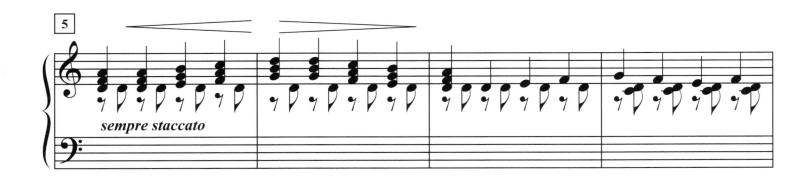

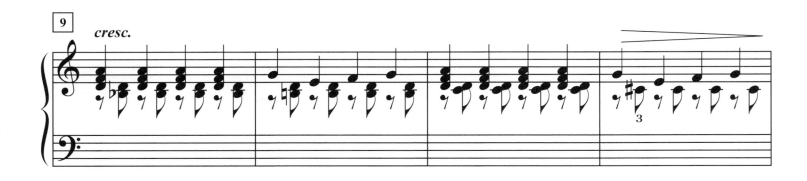

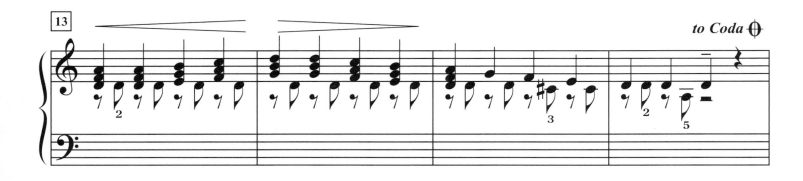

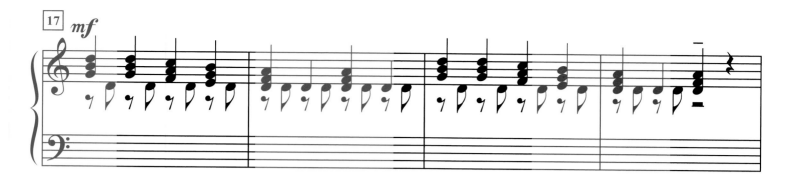

Allegretto Scherzando

Robert D. Vandall

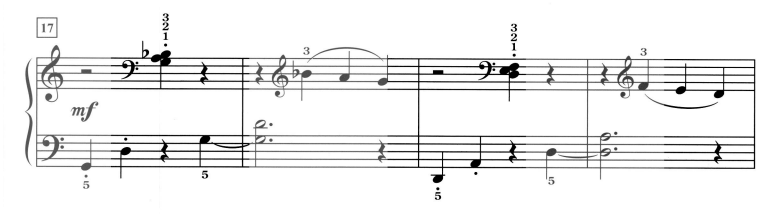

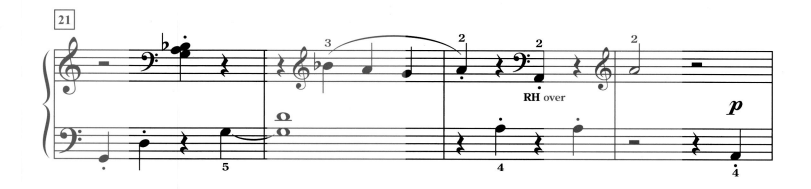

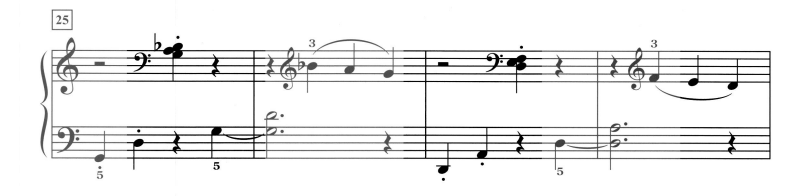

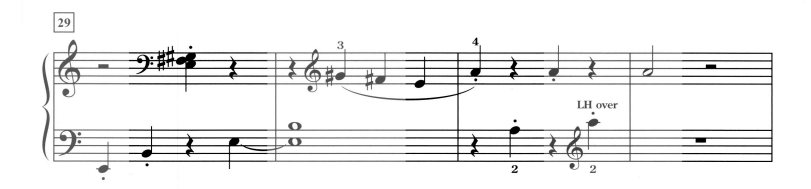

Allegro in A Minor

Robert D. Vandall

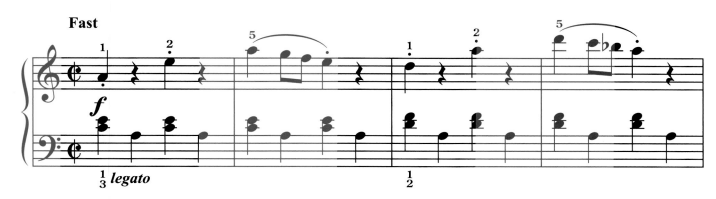

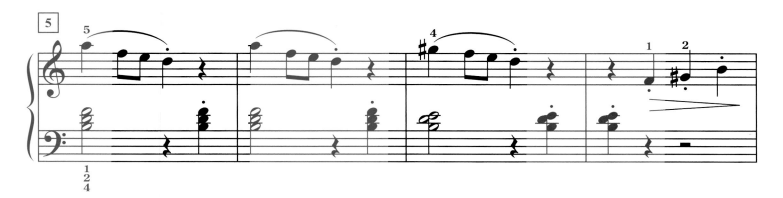

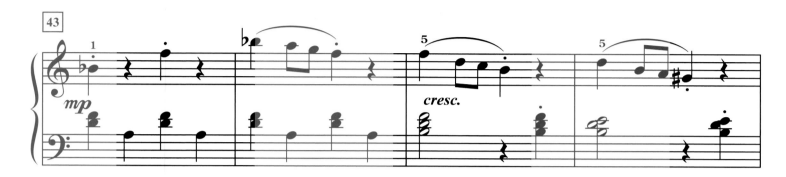

Mystical Tarantella

Robert D. Vandall

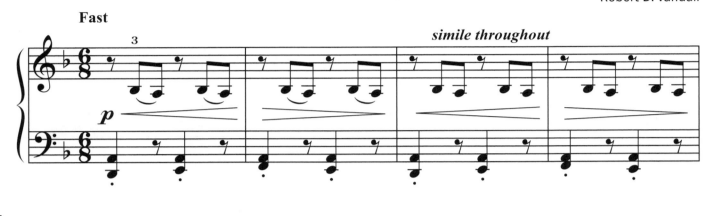

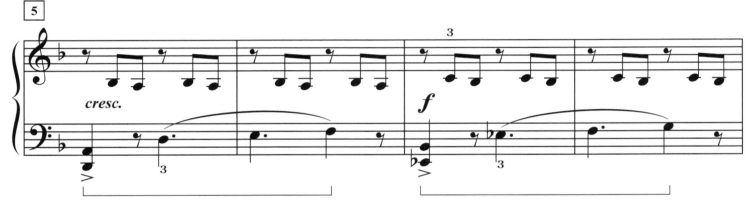

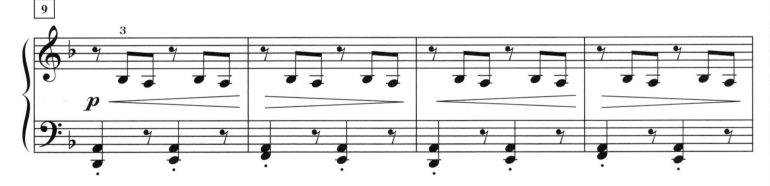

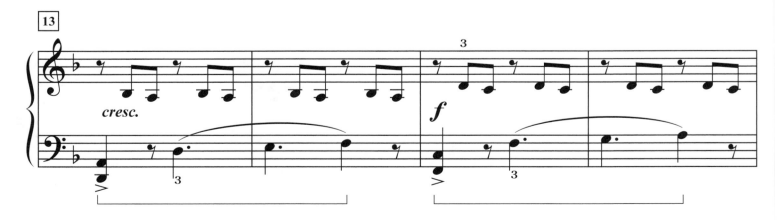

24